Why Leaders Fail

You Won't Be Handed Success Until You Learn How To Handle Failure

Ronald L. Godbee

ISBN-13: 978-1508819189

ISBN-10: 1508819181

Why Leaders Fail

Cover Design by Ruth E. Griffin
Image by Marcos Mesa Sam Wordley/Shutterstock

Scripture quotations taken from The King James Version (Public Domain).

www.ronaldgodbee.net
Email: ronaldgodbee@outlook.com

Printed in U.S.A

DEDICATION

This book is dedicated to every individual who helped me live beyond my failures. My life is a composite of so many wonderful people and valuable experiences. To recall everyone who has been responsible for my development would exceed the word count of this entire book. Thank you for allowing my failures to not determine the final outcome of our friendships.

I'd like to dedicate this book to my wife Karla Godbee. My greatest success was surrendering to the sovereign plan of God and asking you to be my wife. I am only the man I am because you are the woman you are. You married a failing man but through your love, your prayers, and your support, I am a successful husband, a successful father and a successful leader.

CONTENTS

FOREWORD

Albert Schweitzer wisely noted, “In everyone's life, at some time, our inner fire goes out. It is then burst into flame by an encounter with another human being. We should all be thankful for those people who rekindle the inner spirit.”

Pastor Ronald Godbee is one of those persons whom God is using to rekindle the inner spirit of broken, fallen and wounded leaders. Failing is a natural part of succeeding. Just as toddlers fall in the process of learning to walk, so do leaders fail in the process of succeeding. We learn much more from our failures than we do from our successes. There is also something about failing that creates a tenderness in us that empowers us to be compassionate with others who fail.

The greatest value of our failures is what they teach us and what they help us to become as a result. Failure destroys some people while it motivates others. So why is that? It is because they respond to failure differently. How you respond to your failures determines your future! Let your HINDSIGHT give you INSIGHT for how to improve your FORESIGHT!

Godbee’s book does not merely give you the answers to the conundrums of life, but it asks you questions that start the journey of self-discovery. Unless we ask questions, we don’t get answers. Things are not as simple as they appear. All treasure is hidden. We have to dig for it. But eventually we will unearth true treasures that unlock the hurts and failures of our past, and release us into our future.

Though it may appear that destruction and personal failure happen overnight, this is only an illusion. Failure and destruction are GRADUAL and then SUDDEN! The secrets in our lives gradually eat away at our foundation, our principles, our character and our integrity. Then suddenly the floor caves in and the doors fall off their hinges. Cancer attacks the same way—gradually then suddenly.

This book will help to identify the little foxes that destroy the vines in our lives. It is written from a perspective of love, respect and compassion. Love picks us up by our weaknesses, but respect releases us in our strength. Now, may your spirit be rekindled as you process the message of this book. Let the healing begin, and realize that wellness is a process not a procedure.

Bishop Dale C. Bronner
Word of Faith Family Worship Cathedral
Austell, GA

INTRODUCTION

The Right Questions

Many leaders fail because they focus on having the right answers. What they do not understand is that they will be successful only when they discover how to ask the right questions. Questions are important. They are valuable in our pursuit of wisdom. The right questions will lead us to the right answers; and the right answers will lead us to that ancient relic called "truth". Illusive to many, truth is often buried beneath the discord and disharmony of life. It is up to us then to unearth this treasure by asking the questions that will challenge and empower us to face the things we have been avoiding.

'Why Leaders Fail' was written to assist you in asking the hard questions. We often read materials only to arrive at the conclusion of the writer. This book will help you arrive at your own conclusions. However, that can only happen when you are willing to ask yourself the questions poignantly plotted in the course of this reading. Only then will you find the place of self-discovery that will aid you as a leader and help you secure your success.

I have had the distinct privilege of shepherding, mentoring and developing many leaders. Unfortunately, I have also watched with great anguish and pain as prodigious leaders experienced private failures in very public ways. I have been a front-seat witness to the flawed finality of many of our famed leaders. I have beheld their rise to great levels of success, only to end up wasting it all over a reckless incident. I have observed families fall and empires crumble; while great people go from common to king and back to common again. I have retrospectively and introspectively regarded the lives of fallen leaders; and been haunted by their history, wondering about their possibilities: "what-if" they had done this, or "what-if" they had not done that?

Through this, I started seeing a parallel between the leaders of today and those of the biblical writings. I also began to discover strategies in the scriptures that would secure leaders in their reign if they simply took the time to understand them. After all, the scriptures remain not only for our inspiration, information and importation; but as an admonition against what should not be done as well. There is a hidden treasure in the Bible that shows us how to avoid repeating the poor performance of our past predecessors; and as we audit the men of God and discover the "don'ts" of leadership, I think you will be amazed by what we uncover.

The Don'ts of Leadership

There are a number of materials that teach us how to lead but there is very little that sheds light on what we should not do as leaders. Why do great leaders continue to have great failures? It cannot be that they are shortsighted or foolish; and it certainly cannot be that they are not intelligent. They have mastered "the moment" utilizing their intellect, skill sets and competency. Yet it always seems they fail in the simplest and most idiotic ways. If you are like me, your first response to most leaders' failures is *"what in the world were they thinking?"* It is almost as if these great minds took a leave of absence and alleviated themselves of any sense; "*like they were having a buy-one-get-one free sale on stupidity and they were the first in line.*" This is a sarcastic, simple answer but the truth is far more complex. One would hope that it were just a temporary moment where they abandoned all logic and reason, but for many leaders what appears to be an impermanent moment of insanity is really a result of a lifetime of unaddressed issues.

I want to help you uncover the things lying dormant in you that you have yet to confront. I want to assist you in conquering them, so you do not become a part of the *"what were they thinking?"* crew. The has-beens of life are people who at one point were right where you are now. No one took the time to help them discover the things we are going to find in here; but as you read this book, my hope is that you feel we are partnering to pursue what could be a destiny moment for you.

To help us on this journey, we are going to focus on historical figures and their failures: David, Samson, Elijah and Elisha, and Noah. If we are willing to realistically analyze their tenure as great leaders, we will discover where they made their greatest mistakes. The lessons we will extract from their lives are not messages of condemnation but messages of conviction; and as we look at the lives of these great leaders, my prayer is that you are convicted by the things that challenged their leadership.

Because I am a pastor, we are going to expose and scrutinize them in a way they have rarely been viewed. Please do not think I am desecrating any of the great icons of our faith or am in any way disrespecting them - I am a benefactor of the benevolence of God's sacred texts. I am who I am because of his scriptures and those we have come to admire from the hallmark of faith. But I believe God gave us his written record so we could see that the icons of our faith experienced failures and frailties; and so that we could imitate their successes rather than their failures.

To accomplish this, the things covered by romantic language must be unveiled so that we can take a realistic look at their struggles, challenges and difficulties. We must see beyond the leader's genius, strategy and triumph; and discover the chink in their armor. We must analyze not just what *"makes"* a man but what *"breaks"* him as well. The election of a leader is a sovereign thing; this means God's hand is the one that develops us. But if this statement is true, then this means our hand is the one that destroys us. We do not have as much to do with our making but we do have everything to do with the breaking. So it is in our best interest to study the things we can control and leave to God the things he controls.

It is been pointed out many times before and I think it is worth restating: a leader's greatest enemy is not the one he fights outwardly but the one he fights inwardly. The "inner me" is more often than not the true enemy. So let us embark on this journey together and identify the proclivities of great leaders that limit their possibilities. Let us explore the limitless possibilities of your leadership and help you overcome your challenges so you discover a continuous realm of greatness. Let us ask ourselves the tough questions so we may gain the right answers. Let us do all this, so that when people mention your name, they will not follow it up with the question, *"whatever happened to that guy"*?

PART I: DAVID

It Happened When I Was Common

The things that affect us before we become leaders, when we were common, are often the things that destroy us when we finally fill that position - when we, in essence, become king. We think just because we have moved to the mountaintop of our present that we have gotten through the valleys of our yesterday. However, if we do not properly navigate the hurdles of the past, then the things that were designed to challenge and develop us will affect us inwardly and jeopardize our future.

One of my best friends and his wife were expecting their first boy. They were overwhelmed with excitement as I am sure you can imagine. On the day of the birth of their baby, I waited with tiptoe expectancy for a phone call from my friend; but the call never came. Anxious for some news, I called him.

"We ran into some difficulties," he advised me with panic in his voice, then asked me to pray: his son inhaled when he should have exhaled, and he ingested the fluids that had protected him for the last nine months. The fluid that had developed him was now jeopardizing his life.

Similarly many leaders inhale when they should exhale. We ingest things from our past that are fatal to our future. What we were *in* was designed to develop us, not get in us. Yet because it does, we find ourselves on life support, fighting for our lives, as we deal with the predicament of how to lead without bringing the bitterness and brokenness from the past into the present assignment. Our failure to do so will compromise us and cause us to act from a place of dysfunction; and no one epitomizes this more than David. He mismanaged a moment as king, reacting from a common experience and not a king's awareness. Anytime a king resorts to his common knowledge to execute kingly judgment, the results are disastrous.

The Cover-Up

In 2 Samuel 11, we read the story of David's affair with Bathsheba.

> *2 And it came to pass in an eveningtide, that David arose from off his bed, and walked upon the roof of the king's house: and from the roof he saw a woman washing herself; and the woman was very beautiful to look upon. 3 And David sent and enquired after the woman. And one said, Is not this Bathsheba, the daughter of Eliam, the wife of Uriah the Hittite? 4 And David sent messengers, and took her; and she came in unto him, and he lay with her; for she was purified from her uncleanness: and she returned unto her house. 5 And the woman conceived, and sent and told David, and said, I am with child. 6 And David sent to Joab, saying, Send me Uriah the Hittite. And Joab sent Uriah to David. 7 And when Uriah was come unto him, David demanded of him how Joab*

did, and how the people did, and how the war prospered. 8 And David said to Uriah, Go down to thy house, and wash thy feet. And Uriah departed out of the king's house, and there followed him a mess of meat from the king. 9 But Uriah slept at the door of the king's house with all the servants of his lord, and went not down to his house. 10 And when they had told David, saying, Uriah went not down unto his house, David said unto Uriah, Camest thou not from thy journey? why then didst thou not go down unto thine house? 11 And Uriah said unto David, The ark, and Israel, and Judah, abide in tents; and my lord Joab, and the servants of my lord, are encamped in the open fields; shall I then go into mine house, to eat and to drink, and to lie with my wife? as thou livest, and as thy soul liveth, I will not do this thing. 12 And David said to Uriah, Tarry here to day also, and to morrow I will let thee depart. So Uriah abode in Jerusalem that day, and the morrow. 13 And when David had called him, he did eat and drink before him; and he made him drunk: and at even he went out to lie on his bed with the servants of his lord, but went not down to his house. 14 And it came to pass in the morning, that David wrote a letter to Joab, and sent it by the hand of Uriah. 15 And he wrote in the letter, saying, Set ye Uriah in the forefront of the hottest battle, and retire ye from him, that he may be smitten, and die.

At the time when kings went to battle, David remained at home and sent his servants instead. When he should have been battling his enemy, he was at home, succumbing to the lust of his flesh. David allowed himself to get caught up in a moment of weakness; and when Bathsheba sent word of her pregnancy several weeks later, David conspired to cover-up his sins – first by trying to deceive Uriah into sleeping with his wife, then by sending the man to the front line of battle so that he was killed.

As leaders, we must understand it is not the sin that dethrones you, but the cover-up. When you draw from past dysfunctional experiences to deal with present failures, you are going to produce an epic failure. David chose to send Uriah to the front line of battle to be killed because early in his developmental stage, King Saul sent David to do the same. This experience got inside of him when he was common and came back to kill him after he became king. It was David's decision to cover-up his sin that unearthed the thing lying dormant in him; and because he never dealt with the experience, it returned to deal with him.

Most leaders have vowed never to be the oppressor – until they become powerful, and the common situation that was supposed to teach them what not to do is the thing they find themselves doing. The "flesh thing" wars with the "faith thing"; and the conflict becomes how not to do to others what has been done to them. How does the wounded not wound? How does the hurt not hurt?

We are accomplished yet we are left to draw from dysfunctional wells of experience and damaged pasts. We become killers instead of kings; but we are meant to impact others from the throne, not to live out of our past dysfunctions and frustrations.

To accomplish this, we need to identify the issues and open up to those we can trust, those who will hold us accountable for the way we lead and therein secure us in our leadership position.

Peers of the Great

We often brag about our sphere of influence but rarely do we implement a circle of accountability; and if we do, it comes from beneath us rather than over; from a lesser level rather than a greater one. We cannot have people in our sphere of influence who accommodate us in our dysfunctional places, nor can you afford to have a source you are submitted to that supports your flaws. A dysfunctional leader cannot have dysfunctional people as their source of accountability; they then become the proverbial "blind leading the blind". So who are the peers of the great?

Every leader needs a voice they respect speaking into their lives. They need a voice of integrity and wisdom encouraging and challenging them; they need someone they regard as a source of accountability. When Jesus was baptized in the Jordan River, the heavens opened up, the Holy Spirit descended and God spoke (Matthew 3:16-17). He who was on a higher level affirmed the son who was on a lower level; and it was when God confirmed Jesus that he was activated for the assignment.

In addition to activating gifts, affirmation activates our integrity. Integrity is not perfection; it is not what you do. Integrity is how

It is dangerous not to recognize your own dysfunction. This is why integrity is important. Integrity allows us to subject our works to the finality of our flesh, instead of being subjected to the frailties of our flesh. Without the aid of an alibi or excuse for the error, integrity will redirect your flesh-driven pathway. Integrity recognizes your limitations and rescues you from yourself. David covered his flesh with his dysfunctional past when he should have addressed it, confessed it, owned it and corrected it. For that reason, it is important we learn from his mistakes, before our dysfunctional past, left unchecked, kills us.

The Dreams of the Mighty

Likewise lack of integrity will keep you from the greatest desire of your heart. Many leaders are frustrated because they are accomplished in their careers but are being withheld from producing the desire of their hearts. David never wanted to be king; rather, he wanted only to build God a house. The thing he did not ask for he got, but the thing he wanted was withheld from him. Why? Because of his inability to process his past.

This is where "Uriah" comes in. "Uriah" is every leader's opportunity to bury the dysfunctions of their past. It is the chance to process what is in your heart before you do something destructive with your hand. David's sin was not Bathsheba in and of itself. No, his sin was a poor decision, complicated by a wicked cover-up. He reached into his hurt and inflicted his pain on an innocent bystander, killing his dream in the process. When dysfunction contaminates the "faithful", the dreams of the mighty die: how many dreams have you forfeited because of your flesh? Never allow what was on you to get in you - it will keep you from the one thing your heart desires.

Like David, we fail because our past frailties surface in our present realities. Our strength is diluted by the devious acts that were perpetrated against us in our vulnerable years; and as we grew up, our schoolmaster became the dysfunction of our forefathers, a subject we will further explore when we talk about the relationship between Elijah and Elisha. Of course, if we knew the abuse, torment and anguish our leaders have endured to get where they are, we would do more to repair and heal them rather than judge them. But because we make more money destroying instead of uplifting them, we allow great gifts to be thrown away based upon bad behaviors. We lift people up to tear them down because it is our way of acknowledging and dealing with our own personal dysfunctions.

If this pattern continues we will see more leaders opt out of publicly displaying their gifts. How about we heal the hurting, repair the broken and stand ready to help our fallen soldiers instead? This is not tolerance but an opportunity to preserve genius. Who would dare to be great if the end result was their demise at the hands of those they seek to serve? We must create an environment to ensure our "accomplished" leaders we will get them help for their past so society can benefit from their future. We must train to reign, so that our greatest boast is not that we did too little as a community to keep our leaders standing. Otherwise, we will continue to see the tragedy of David and Uriah unfold on a daily basis.

"Re-create" not Rehabilitate

You never know who you are until you are poor enough or powerful enough to expose the perversion of humanity. It is this mixture – the elixir of poverty and the intoxicant of power – that reveals our true identity. But we need not be taken aback when the individual in the seat of authority is uncovered. Once we discover their deficiency, we need to "re-create" the leader, not rehabilitate them. To rehabilitate someone is to "re-habit" them, and take them back to the origin of their experience or "habit", but this is to make the assumption their former habits were proper. The truth is someone's reckless behavior is an indication that they have been improperly indoctrinated with the wrong habits. As educated as most leaders are, we need to reeducate and help them learn habits that are necessary for a successful reign as a leader.

I Samuel 18:17 And Saul said to David, Behold my elder daughter Merab, her will I give thee to wife: only be thou valiant for me, and fight the Lord's battles. For Saul said, Let not mine hand be upon him, but let the hand of the Philistines be upon him.

In this verse, we find Saul plotting David's death, much like David planned Uriah's. It was at this point, when he was fighting Saul's machinations against him, that David's vice began. We talk about generational curses but never take time to discover generational vices. The curse is a transfer through blood but generational vices come from an impartation of negligent leaders. Every leader's dysfunction can be traced back to a dysfunctional leader who mismanaged their opportunity to properly develop them. The fathers who are supposed to protect us are the ones desiring to kill us, cognitively transmitting their bitterness, only to have this cycle play itself out later, with us in the role of leadership destroying yet another generation of leaders.

It is extremely traumatic to find out the one whom you are most impressed with is the one trying to kill you because they are intimidated by you. But when the role is reversed and you are in the position of king, will you choose to repeat what was done to you? At some point every leader must discover their toxic place and commit to never impose that problem on another person.

Are you intimidated by upcoming leaders? How many generations will be damaged by our fear of their advancement? We are supposed to prepare the next generation to reign; instead we are contaminating them with toxic experiences that will come back later to haunt them. We are to give "advice", not "to add a vice". As advisors we are expected to provide opportunities for advancement, not jeopardize the lives of emerging generations. It is easy to blame young leaders for their dysfunctions but the truth is many of them are byproducts of a contaminated generation. Every predecessor must take ownership of their responsibility to cultivate the ones who will come after them. After all, they could be the next king. How you handle them now may determine how they reign later.

Suppression is the enemy of deliverance

We have heard the saying, "the inner me is the enemy". Now let us dissect it and see what we are really saying when we make this statement. As leaders, we learn to cope with what we are called to deal with and kill. We suppress and mask it with a disguise called work, medicating ourselves with anything but the real thing. We develop and devise mechanisms that help us hide; and we call it our strength. But what we perceive as strength is actually our greatest weakness. It is an escape; something we are running from. We work around it, accomplish through it and build upon it but we never get delivered from it.

The enemy would have us believe keeping it under control is sufficient. We hold it down, and believe we are "strong". We accept our achievements as confirmation that we are getting better. But we are not: inwardly we are growing worse. Regardless of our victories, we are being victimized by our vices. We can hold them down until both our hands get full, but now we are too busy to bother with the burden of our vices. We cannot keep our vices down while trying to keep our victories up.

It is said "idle hands are the devil's workshop", but busy hands are the place where the enemy blindsides you. You cannot see the attack coming when you are consumed with going forward. Full hands incapacitate and render you helpless against the voracious appetite of your vice. So now you are trying to manage the vice that is trying to come up because you know if it does, it is going to bring you down. It rears its ugly head and you push it back down, believing it is fixed. We are famous for suppressing, and choosing not to deal with underlying issues, except on a "have-to" basis. But as soon as the rush and list of accomplishments are satisfied, instead of getting victory over our vices we find we have given victory to our vices.

Courage to Confront

Most leaders are motivated by the sound of the crowd. They fall prey to the proclivities of their flesh because they become intoxicated by the sounds of success, but as long as we hear the crowd, we quell the sound of our vices calling us. For many of us, we have never experienced the accoutrement of leadership. The attractiveness of the anointing attracts both good and bad. It awakens the sleeping giant within. This is something every leader must understand: the sleeping giant can be awakened. What is your sleeping giant? If you do not know what it is and your adversary does, you are already defeated. Every leader must be clear that there is someone or something that can bring you down. Do not ever sleep on what can be awakened in your life.

Just because you have gotten over something does not mean you are done with it. Many leaders find they have the strength to move on, but not the courage to confront what they are moving on from. Sometimes "keeping it moving" will come back to haunt you and destroy your destiny. This is why it is important for us to not allow our movement to become our moment of masking.

David faced his own giant by the name of Goliath (1 Samuel 17:4-51), but he did not just knock him out; he also stood on the giant's chest and cut off his head. A knockdown does not defeat Goliath. Many leaders need the wisdom of David to come closer and face the thing they knocked out at a distance. What have you knocked out that you need to go back and cut off?

We must go into the dark places of our lives, the place where the enemy tried to stop our development, where our lives were threatened while we are unable to fend for ourselves and deal with it. When Jesus was still a child, King Herod issued a decree for all babies to be killed (Matthew 2:3-16) because he was intimidated by Jesus and the greatness he possessed. Every leader must uncover the attack launched against them in their infancy and address the assault on their anointing if they are to find success. Otherwise, what Herod did not do to us, we will end up doing to ourselves.

It is vitally important to understand and identify those who tried to hinder you so you do not hurt those who are trying to help you. Sadly, most leaders end up in this position, where they hurt those who are there to help them, because they carry the baggage of those who tried to hurt *them.* They suffer because of what was done to them in their stages of immaturity; and now that they are mature, they subconsciously seek revenge for those who damaged them when they could not defend themselves. This results in leaders having the inability to interact with others on a personal level or engage in an intimate way. We blame our lack of sensitivity on our drive to be an *accomplished leader* but it is the memories of those who tried to kill us when we were most vulnerable that prevent us from making that connection.

Every leader should understand that the enemy has three stages of attack: first, he tries to kill you in your infant stage. Secondly, he attempts to conflict you in the wilderness; and thirdly, he tries to confuse you in the garden. Let us look at these further in-depth.

Purpose

The first stage of attack happens when you are in your infant stage. When you are attacked in your infancy you have two choices; you can become bitter or emboldened. When you understand God protected your purpose, bitterness will not be an option. He defends those who cannot defend themselves so destiny is assured in spite of what was done to you. The things etched in you should be the affirmation of your awesomeness and not your reason to revert to becoming what you despise.

Leaders need to process and purify each stage of their lives before moving into their next phase of success. Do not allow your adolescent obstacles to eclipse your accomplishments in the adult world. If you are ever going to attract the sustaining power of God, you must outgrow the attacks that took place in your immature stages. You cannot progress and regress at the same time: a successful person who is progressing in their career but regressing in their personal life is a house divided against itself.

In this stage, Herod stands as a metaphor in our lives. Our enemies are aware of who we are before we realize it; but if they could not kill you then, they certainly cannot kill you now. Never give up what you gained because you chose to go back to places that God protected you in. They could not injure you when you were immature so be mature enough to outlive the things that were done. Do not die by the sword of another man's ignorance.

Strength

The second stage of the enemy's attack transpires in the wilderness, where he seeks to conflict you. It is often preached that Jesus was at his weakest when he went into the wilderness, but I would like to submit that he was at his strongest. God will never allow you to go into the wilderness at your weakest. Most leaders do not understand the purpose of the wilderness: it is a place of recovery, a place for the powerful not the powerless. The wilderness was where Christ reestablished the patterns of the garden and where we regain everything we gave up. The wilderness is not for wimps, it is for warriors. It is the place where we defeat every temptation and overcome every obstacle; where your hunger teaches you that man shall not live by bread alone but by every word that precedes from the mouth of God (Matthew 4:4); where man becomes profoundly aware of his dependence upon God as his source. The wilderness is an opportunity to crucify your flesh and fortify your relationship with God.

Most leaders, however, do the antithesis: they get in the wilderness and give into their flesh. We cannot afford to get to the place where victory is to be found and we succumb to our frailties. I believe if we would just identify the purpose of the wilderness, we will be better prepared to face its challenge and exit with total victory. This is not the time for conflict to reign in your members but for you to concretize your faith.

If you are in your wilderness, you are there on purpose. Jesus was led into the wilderness by the Holy Spirit (Mark 1:12) and you are no different. You are in this place not because you have been bad but because you have been led; because God in his sovereign power is saying you are strong enough to defeat the very thing that has been defeating you. Never despise the wilderness experience. When you learn how to work your wilderness, you will learn how to overcome your weaknesses.

Crossroads

For the third stage, the enemy brings us to the garden. Like Christ in the Garden of Gethsemane, we come to a crossroads: we either move forward into our purpose or become paralyzed by the possibilities. It is in the garden most leaders give up on their destiny. The possibilities of the unknown keep us from pursuing everything God placed us in the earth to go after. It is at the crossroad that our divinity begins to struggle with our humanity: our greatness is challenged by our weakness and we hemorrhage at the idea of doing something we have never done before.

Most leaders fail because of their fear of going forward. The possibilities are unfathomable, so they forfeit their identity and go in the opposite direction. They abandon their mission when conflicted by their choices and discover that the garden, a pretty place, is also a dangerous one.

So how do we accomplish that which we have never done before? Fear drives us into areas of uncertainty; it produces perversion and we who are carnal are not always able to overcome it, falling prey to it instead. How do we die to the fear that confines us to our proverbial cross? Christ being the pattern son shows us how to overcome fear. How did Christ die? How did eternity wrapped in finite flesh confine himself to a cross and experience something he had never experienced before (death)?

We find the answers to those questions when we answer another question: what (or where) is your pretty place? The garden, the pretty place, is a place of conflict. In the garden you have to go beyond your support systems to something unfamiliar. Moreover, you realize that not everyone has your belief system, can pray with you and last as long as you can.

But it is also in the garden we find the opportunity to give in and surrender to choice. For you see, the mark of power is your ability to now choose. As Christ had to choose his divinity over his humanity, you and I are given an opportunity to choose our divinity over our humanity. Which will reign when it is your turn to choose? Will your choices be divine or carnal?

Prior to possessing power, choices were limited. Anyone can be morally absent of choice; but morality only becomes evident when one has the opportunity to be immoral. It is at the crossroads when the fabric of your faith is being pulled that you find out what your foundational truths are. Core values become evident. When you can afford to be immoral but you make a choice to remain moral, then you truly know morality exists in you.

Every leader needs to understand that they are established at the crossroads of life. Character without a junction is like a tree falling in the forest with no one there to hear: whether it makes a sound or not, without someone present to appreciate it, the action becomes pointless. If we understand the purpose of the garden, we can intentionally pursue our core values and maintain our ethical benchmarks. Then when we are afforded the opportunity to give testimony of our character, our choices will speak louder than our words. This is not your time to be conflicted; it is your time to move in your convictions.

Convictions

Every leader needs to understand their convictions. Like Christ, we must be confronted with the challenge of the garden so that we are fortified in our faith and sold out to our core values. Any leader who has not established his or her core values will always fail the test of the garden.

Have you failed your garden test? If you have, it is probably because you have been leading without ethics or core values. The beauty of grace is that in the garden we have a chance to discover or rediscover the foundation from whence we stand. Your triumph comes in the decisions you make, not in the territory you take. Every leader needs to have a Gethsemane experience so as to fortify their foundation and focus on the real missions of life. Christ could conquer his garden and go to his cross because he understood what came after his death. Had he not decided to die, he would have never experienced his resurrection; and this is a choice all leaders must understand: the way to life is through death. The pathway to a successful life is achieved through a decision to die to our natural flesh. The hard choice becomes easy when I understand what comes next. As leaders we are able to foresee, therefore we should understand that to die is to gain.

Our choices do matter. We cannot effectively change and transform our corporations, our finances and our families without factoring in our futures. We must foresee our future and make decisions today based on what we see in our tomorrow. When making a decision, any leader who does not forecast his future is a fool to move forward in that decision. Your future will reflect the choice you made in your crossroads. Right now you are the sum total of the choices you made at your point of conflict. What choice will you make about your future and who will it affect?

We often say God has grace for all our sins, and he does, but people do not. God is graceful, but people are not. God will forgive you but family, friends and finances will not. The choices you make will determine the relationship you forsake. When you make the wrong choice, you affect the right people. It is incumbent upon each of us when we come to our crossroads to choose the things that will enhance our family, enrich our relationships and ensure our success.

The Cross

We are not fighting for our salvation or our souls; we are fighting for the sustainability of our success. True deliverance is taking ownership of the opportunity to publicly crucifying the thing that causes you a private crisis. Similar to what Christ did on the cross at Calvary, we must endure our cross and despise our shame in order to receive our crown of righteousness. Stop believing you have gotten past the thing you have not died from. Until you die to it, you will never truly experience the fullness of the life that God wants you to have.

Unfortunately, today's leaders do not know how to die on the cross. Can you imagine the conflict of the Christ? How does the source of life die? How does a successful person face the areas they are not successful in? If a leader is going to conquer the things designed to stop them, they must be willing to die to them. They must carry their sins to their personal place of crucifixion and deal with them there.

If you do not confront what you have not dealt with, please know it lives to kill you. Therefore you must intentionally approach it before it destroys you. To do this, you need to fixate on the thing that seeks to forfeit your destiny and destroy it. What sleeping Giants need to be dealt with inside of you? What crucifixion needs to take place that could be used to help save the world?

The greatest accountability and assurance of deliverance is one which takes place in public. If you are the Christ, at some point your private battle must be placed on public display; and if you have an objective of saving the public, you must be made vulnerable to them. They must see the areas where you die so they too can join you in death. The cross is an invitation to come and die with the Christ. It is a clarion call issued from the cross for all humanity to die to their sin nature.

With a public display of private pain, every leader has an opportunity to invite people to die in the place the leader died. Could you imagine everyone who could be saved? By showing their wounds and their scars like the apostle Thomas did, those who experience similar pain might believe.

I love the story of Thomas. We often call him "Doubting Thomas", but we must be careful with the tags and titles we place on people. Thomas was not a doubter, but someone who wanted to believe. He heard the stories of Christ's resurrection and wanted to personally experience it himself. He told the other disciples, "Except I have seen what you saw and experienced what you have experienced, I cannot believe like you believe (John 20:25)." Jesus' response to him showed how much he loved him: he appeared to Thomas and gave him the same opportunity as the other ten disciples. He told him to touch the places he had been wounded and hurt most.

Christ was not afraid to expose himself in the areas he had been victimized and was most vulnerable in; and because of this experience, Thomas was able to believe on the same level as the other disciples. As leaders, we pray the public is never made privy to our painful places; but if Christ is to be our example, then we should take advantage of every opportunity to expose our pain so others might believe.

Tell on Yourself

Being a leader does not mean being absent of flaws; on the contrary, it means having the ability to overcome flaws. Why then are we so ashamed to expose our strength of overcoming? The Word of God states we are overcomers by the blood of the Lamb and by the word of our testimony (Revelations 12:11). The strength of every leader is that we have lived through the painful place. We have overcome the nails in our hands and feet, and the wounds in our side. We must stand ready to ask people to touch the places where we hurt the most.

My dad gave me a great piece of advice growing up: tell on yourself. It is hard for people to hold you hostage when you are the one who has disclosed the thing causing you discomfort. But most leaders do not get delivered because they keep dirty, little secrets. It is the keeping of these secrets that precludes us from helping others who struggle with the same issues we do. We are called from among them, but if no one knows what you are struggling with, how can they know you are no longer dealing with it? The Bible says, "Confess your sins one to another (James 5:16)." Why? If I know what you are struggling with, I can partner with you to kill it before it kills you. Public accountability is powerful. It creates a circle of influence that sustains us in the finished work of the cross.

Many of us choose to suppress our sin because we like the idea of getting past it until we can get back to it. But real deliverance is in taking away that power. Paul said, "I die daily (1 Corinthians 15:31)." So every leader must die daily to his flesh, to bring about public accountability where we can serve our fellow man and not our flawed, finite flesh.

Suppression is for the mediocre, not the great. Great men and women have a great awareness of the areas they need to grow in. Instead of allowing our constituency the opportunity to operate under the myth that we are superhuman, we need to do a better job of connecting them to our humanity and continually reminding people we are *all* in route to being the best "self" possible.

For this reason, we need to afford leaders the opportunity to grow to their day of deliverance. The garden and the crossroads are the pathways to development. We must allow every leader those two purposeful places before we disqualify them based upon behaviors they have yet to be delivered from. This is in no way an excuse but simply an opportunity for great leaders to grow into great people.

Nobody Asked Me

Most leaders are like David: they are anointed but not asked. David was simply working in his father's field, tending to his father's sheep. He did not ask to be king, but he was chosen for it. As a leader, I am earmarked for my ability to perform; I am appointed to an assignment without prior consultation. The oil flows on my head but no one asked me if I wanted to be singled out or if I desired to be selected.

As leaders, we are diligent in our efforts and accomplished in the field but often times, we are not prepared for what our abilities attract. Just because I desire to do what I am good at does not mean I have asked to become a model for the world. In our society, we ask people who are proficient at a skill or an art to be perfect in all areas. If we were to ask David who he was, I believe he would have said, "I tend to sheep; and kill bears, lions and giants." He might have also added, "I love God but I did not ask to be the carrier of the community. I did not ask to be put under the microscope of scrutiny to have my life analyzed for centuries to come." David never intended on becoming the center of theological dogma; he just did what he was gifted to do and in doing so, became a specimen and spectacle for all humanity to judge.

David practiced his craft by working his "slingshot game". It prepared him for his assignment, but not the other areas of his life. His preparation never challenged him to train his character. As leaders, we are trained to achieve and master our gifts; however, we are not taught to destroy or deal with our dysfunctions. We cater to what is right, leaving what is wrong to brood and breed. We have a "slingshot mentality" – we work on our aim and never prepare for the fame our aim will bring. Like David, many leaders are proficient at fighting the giants without but they have not conquered the giants within. We have mastered the beast without - the lions, bears and giants - but not the beast within.

In my estimation, the demands we put on common people in kingly roles is unfair. Most leaders never ask to be in charge, they just want to be good at what they do. Who would have thought throwing a rock would take David from the field to the throne? But it did...it landed him in the palace, despite the fact that no one asked him if this is what he wanted. God controlled his destiny – and at times, so did the people around him.

Very few plan for success because they do not have a plan that factors in their flaws. The achiever only acknowledges the favor but never the challenge to own their flaws. The gift is obvious so we go with what we see, but many of us never prepare for what we could be. The true plan for success factors in the flaws of the leader and goes to great lengths to correct the flaws before the reign. The one who prepares for success deals with the things that could compromise all he has worked to accomplish.

The Oil

The call to leadership is extremely difficult because its first assignment is to segregate you from family and set you apart from others. As the anointed and future king, the oil flowed onto David's head, but it refused to acknowledge his brothers.

Well hey, I like my brothers and I never asked to be acknowledged over them; but my heart is unknown to those whom I have given my heart to, making me misunderstood by my family and those close to me. So why does the oil flow on me, but not them? Why am I the one left to deal with the family betrayal, while they wonder why they weren't anointed for the assignment? Why am I the one being picked out to be picked on? I did not ask to be different!

Why can we not accept the dysfunctions of people who are proficient in one area but fail in others? If we understood the price leaders paid in their private family lives before they made it to the public spotlight, we would be more sympathetic. Service of others sometimes separates you from the service of those who love you and need you the most - your family. In my personal life, I watched my brother as he was selected to stand head and shoulders above the rest and anointed for his assignment. But his calling consumed him, taking him away from everyone he loved and everyone who loved him. Holidays, nights, significant events – they were all spent serving others. Then when he experienced a moral frailty and a family failure, those whom he served dismissed him because they believed he was exhibiting a lack of character. He had forfeited his family long before the failure was evident. He had lost his family in private and they were witnessing the results in public.

While most leaders are perfecting their craft, they are losing cherished company. The psychological distinction they suffer before they enter the door of success is difficult. No one asked David if he wanted to leave his family for the unfamiliar, but it was a prerequisite to the throne, a fear he had to overcome if he was to succeed. We may be accomplished as leaders, but it does not mean we do not have fears. We assume because David fought bears, lions and giants he was fearless, but I submit we are fearless only for what we are anointed to do. I can face the bears, the lions and the giants and defeat them without fear, but I cannot face my personal issues alone. Leadership isolates us and causes us to face a life we are not equipped for by ourselves.

Like David, our gifts take us away from the father's house and those who know us best, leaving us to fight with a king who does not have the capacity to father us. We are only in the palace to learn its protocols but doing so does not resolve our personal challenges. Now we are operating in a world absent of those who understand us and could help us. Now the public scrutinizes our private life in public only because of our desire to serve; and to top it off our family life was done before the spotlight ever hit us.

The paradox of being anointed is that we are anointed for others but not for ourselves. How do we discover us when we have always lived for others? We are anointed to stop things from destroying others, but who is there to stop the bears and giants from attacking us? We only wanted to make a difference not to become a target. We should be surrounded by supporters but instead we have only attracted attackers. The assignment takes more than it gives and no one asked us if we wanted to give our lives.

We are never told that signing on the dotted line hands over our lives not just our gifts. Somewhere in the fine print of the covenant you are contracted to benefit the contractor. This leaves many leaders to ask "what in the world did I sign up for?" No one tells the truth about the perils and pitfalls of acquiring something you were gifted for but not mentally prepared for. We need to spend more time developing our "mental game" instead of our "slingshot game". We need counseling for our family "effects". We need to be honest about what fuels our fire and what we are fighting.

The world wants you to be all things even though you only wanted to be one thing. A recording artist wants to sing, an athlete wants to play, a writer wants to write and David only wanted to work for his father. David's gift took him away from what he wanted and made him who they thought he should be. No one asked David if he wanted to be king, so why should you expect to be asked?

Common Kills Kings

Admittedly, there are probably more common attributes in me than kingly ones. We all start off as common and being common is not a bad thing. It only becomes problematic when it is brought into positions of priority. The things the common people do every day are unbecoming for the king. So what do I do when my propensities towards the common conflicts with my role of being king? Although I can speak the King's English, I prefer common conversations. Similarly, I can eat at the King's table but I love the food of the common. So how do I overcome what I have been for so long? How do I make the shift? How do I master this monster that is seeking to consume me?

Like a doctor treating an aggressive cancer, we must attack the common and disconnect from it before it compromises our greatness. We cannot remove so much of it that there is no remembrance of it, for our ministry depends on it, but it is essential we allow the cure to work so our bodies can live. It is essential we submit to treatment. In a situation like this, a doctor would prescribe chemotherapy. Chemotherapy is a poison injected into the body to target the cancer and eradicate it. In order to remove all that is adverse and advancing rapidly beyond normalcy, we too must intentionally target the cancer - in this case, the common, because when too many normal things are advancing against you, then the leader in you is in grave danger. Chemotherapy targets bad cells but sometimes the good cells die. But the good cells come back while the bad cells remain gone forever. Praise God!

Let us look at sexual addiction, for example. Sex is common and normal; however when it rapidly advances beyond its limits, it becomes a dysfunction; and when that which is deemed normal by the common is now declared to be dysfunctional when done by uncommon people, then the common majority finds ways to condemn an uncommon minorities' adverse behavior. This is why our newspapers sell: stories are "tabloid-rized" and magazines become tools that demonize our leaders. If the leader is going to keep his success from becoming a spectacle, he must not immerse himself in a rapidly advanced dysfunctional state. The intrigue of the common is not to see the failures of the uncommon leader; but to see themselves in a rapidly advanced, adverse, unhealthy condition in the uncommon leader is their issue. People who follow you do not mind you being different; they just do not want you to be dysfunctional. They do not want a rapidly advancing, adverse version of themselves at the helm of their ship.

Leaders must learn the discipline and art of destroying addictions and attractions. Our accomplishments mean nothing otherwise. Leaders fall when they fail to dominate the undisciplined side of themselves and remove the temptation of being like everyone else. I have often stated married people need to hang out with married people, while single people need to hang out with single people, so their relationships may flourish and they may avoid temptation. Of course there are exceptions to every rule but if the relationship is to be a healthy one, we need to follow rules. Likewise leaders should hang out with their peers. It is the equivalent of chemo killing the cancer so the body can live.

Leaders of organizations need to target the common connections that keep them from being an uncommon leader. Jesus loved the common man; he identified with him and redeemed him, but when Peter got too common he rebuked him (Mark 8:33). Who do you need to cut off to keep you from reconnecting to the familiar part of you? What do you need to change in order to encourage a successful reign as leader? Change in diet, regimen, routine, mindset or behavior - sometimes the most aggressive forms of cancer call for the most radical treatments. Jesus said if your eye offends you pluck it out (Matthew 5:29) - a very practical but radical way to kill an impractical and ridiculous behavior.

Battle Scars

Please understand the severity of your actions and continued attachment to the common things: they will kill your career quicker than anything in the drugstore. It is not unlike suicide by a cop. An individual seeks to end their life but is too afraid to do it by their own hand. They bait a police officer into an aggressive situation and then act as if they are pointing a weapon at them. Officers are trained to protect and defend, and in a situation like this, they are left with only one solution: to fire upon the individual posing the threat. In many instances, the end result is death.

I wonder how many of us are pulling the proverbial gun at life to kill our careers. We are tired of "life as usual", so we live our lives praying someone will shoot and end it all. Most suicide victims do not want to die; rather, they just want an end to the pain. Many leaders are the same: they do not want to not be uncommon, but the pain of being different drives most leaders to yearn for normalcy.

Aggressive actions are our way of opting out. No one explained or helped us process the pain of leading. Everyone celebrates the trailblazer, but no one knows the burns suffered by blazing the trail. The heat of the fire affects the one forging the trail. Conventional wisdom tells us not to touch fire. The first time demonstrates its force; it is so fierce; few want to face it twice and it is at this point, many leaders act out to opt out.

When I was young, I played with some "kid-friendly" sparkles. No boom or bang, just glittering fire. I remember I was so mesmerized by the sparkle, I grabbed it at its core and burned my hand. The pain was so intense, I "opted out" of playing with sparkles afterward. To this day, I have never used, nor have I allowed my children to play with sparkles. They have missed the beauty of seeing this spectacle all because of my experience at the age of five. Instead of teaching my children how to properly handle a sparkle, I mismanaged my opportunity to train them for the experience.

Burns can prevent you from future productivity as well as interfere with the next generations' ability to benefit from the place where you had a bad experience. Never underestimate the power of your burns. I did not realize how deeply it affected me until I began writing this some 38 years later.

As I recall, the pain was exacerbated because of home remedies and old wives tales. My mom put butter on the burn and we cringe at that today because we know better, but at the time she did what she believed was best. I submit many are doing the same today: you are using homemade remedies on your burns, aggravating the condition and worsening the experience. Burns are painful enough - the cure should not make your situation worse.

Whether intentional or done out of ignorance, we wind up doing more harm than good when we seek relief from our burns through alternative avenues that are not God-based. We end up doing bad things not because we are bad people but because we believe what we do will heal our pain. My mom is one of the greatest Christian ladies to ever live, but she was void of a viable remedy. So she employed an old wives remedy, inadvertently delaying the healing process and leaving me with an aversion to sparkles. Butter goes well on a baked potato but not a five-year-old's burnt hand.

The endurance of a leader has to be great but the threshold for pain has to be greater. I want to believe we are the benefactors of our position, but more times than not, we are the ones who suffer the most: our greatest victories become our greatest scars and the price of our successes is prominently tattooed onto our flesh. As a leader, take a moment to reflect on the cost of your accomplishments and the price to be in the position you are in. You are great because you have tolerated the things others would have never been able to bear, but you must be willing to tend to the pain you have endured, or you will continue exaggerating your injury.

PART II: SAMSON

Different

We have looked at David and his rise from the common, but as we take Samson into consideration in our bid to understand why leaders fail, it would do us well to recognize that at some point we must not only recognize the common in our leaders and in ourselves, but must also defend against the desire to be normal. We must become comfortable with being different; and as we track the life of Samson, we will discover some of the difficulties of being a unique leader as well as the challenges that make them abort their mission. Let us begin this section by introducing Samson and identifying the issue that brought about his downfall.

Judges 14:3 And the angel of the Lord appeared unto the woman, and said unto her, Behold now, thou art barren, and bearest not: but thou shalt conceive, and bear a son. 4 Now therefore beware, I pray thee, and drink not wine nor strong drink, and eat not any unclean thing: 5 For, lo, thou shalt conceive, and bear a son; and no razor shall come on his head: for the child shall be a Nazarite unto God from the womb: and he shall begin to deliver Israel out of the hand of the Philistines.

Most people benefit from the bare-hand conflicts, baggages of betrayal and battle wounds their leaders fight. However we neglect to recognize the sacrifices they make for the good of society.

These sacrifices weigh on them; and oftentimes the thing identifying them as different becomes the thing they want to separate themselves from. It is at that juncture when the leader sabotages their success in an effort to return to normalcy.

Samson's hair uniquely earmarked him as someone different; but different is not always better to someone who wants to be the same as everyone else. Like Samson, our hair is the symbol of our talent, our gift or in spiritual language, "our anointing". It is the thing that identifies us as different. If we analyze gifted people, we will find they are the loneliest, most isolated and misunderstood people in our society because of their differences. But this is to be expected: the anointing segregates and separates us from those we are fighting for; and most leaders are never made aware of this.

Instead, they assume that the people they are using their gifts for should return the favor by appreciating them but this rarely happens. It would do leaders well to divest themselves of the need to be applauded by the people they serve. They should also understand they are leaders for a reason; and though they are there for the benefit of their followers, leadership may cause others to fear, despise and even betray them. Leaders must become acquainted with this ideal because in many cases it is par for course. It was for Samson, but because he was not developed enough to deal with it, he sabotaged his own success, divorced himself from his destiny and precluded himself from fulfilling his purpose.

The Cost of Battle

In Judges, Chapter 14, we see the journey of the select begin to unfold:

5 Then went Samson down, and his father and his mother, to Timnath, and came to the vineyards of Timnath: and, behold, a young lion roared against him. 6 And the Spirit of the Lord came mightily upon him, and he rent him as he would have rent a kid, and he had nothing in his hand.

Samson comes into the world with an identifying mark that automatically bespeaks of his headship. Headship is a heavy burden because it comes with an identity of its own. You are automatically picked out to be picked on. Samson's hair set him apart in a culture where men did not have long hair. He was distinctively different but he had to be if he was going to deliver God's people. He carried in him the anointing of God to accomplish this; however, what most people do not understand is the anointing attracts the attack. Samson found this out early on in his journey. We brag about his battles won, his triumphant and valiant victories but we do not see the battles from his vantage point. We see the success, the laurels and the defeated enemy, but we miss the scars of the one who succeeded. Most leaders are identified by their victories but no one takes time to explore the psychological backdrop and baggage that attaches itself to them in the midst of the battle.

Everyone celebrates the fact that Samson destroyed a lion with his bare hands, but we fail to comprehend the range of emotions he experienced while being attacked. What went through his head as he tussled and wrestled with the lion? I am sure the level of uncertainty he experienced at some point in his struggle must have been overwhelming. Seconds seemed like hours and hours felt like days, as Samson battled the ferocious, dominating beast proficient at killing its prey. How much damage did it cause before Samson finally killed it? How many bite marks and gashes did it inflict upon the man of God before Samson got the best of it?

The leader is not only different because of his "hair" - his anointing - but because of his ability to persevere. Perseverance within itself states the individual has endured dramatic and traumatic situations that, in many cases, would have taken the average person's life. The victories we celebrate are moments leaders were *forced* to be heroes. Instances we herald as dreams may in fact represent their nightmares. When we realize the violence that has gone into developing these great visionaries, we will stop lauding their fight and start sympathizing with their struggle. We must not only look at what was won but what was endured in order to win.

The Anointing

Samson was anointed, but he was also attacked. This is something every leader must factor in: the attack the anointing attracts. Unfortunately you do not get one without the other. The Christian community portrays the anointing as an accolade, but it is the exact opposite: it is an acknowledgment that you are clothed for the assignment - one that will take you into devastating places to do difficult things and rescue helpless people from hopeless situations. The anointing assigns you to dysfunctional people, deplorable places and dangerous assignments. David had to defeat a giant while the prophet Daniel had to go into a lion's den (Daniel 6:16). Likewise, Samson had to fight a lion. These were places and fights that were difficult and dangerous, brought about by the anointing they carried.

The anointing is attractive to those who do not have it, but to those who are anointed, the anointing can sometimes be annoying. It can be the thing that places you amongst people you had no intention to be around, in places you had no desire to be in and on assignments you never would have selected for yourself. The anointing is not all it is cracked up to be: yes, it opened the eyes of the blind, but those same eyes watched the Christ die on the cross. It provided wine at the wedding at Cana, only to bring thirst to Christ while he languished on the cross. It allowed lame legs to walk – directly to the hillside of Golgotha, where Christ was crucified. While the anointing works for others, it appears to work against the one who is carrying it.

I do not say all this to make you fearful of the anointing but it is important to understand the residual effects from it. The anointing is powerful enough to change lives, but often results in leaders opting out of their assignments to tend to the wounds they incurred in battle. We celebrate their victories, but neglect their hurts; and for Samson, the lion was just one encounter. How many other battles were there? For every battle seen, we can assume there are equal battles unseen. For every beast that brings the leader fame, we can presuppose there are others which leave deeper, grotesque scars. The sum total of a leader's existence is comprised of what we know about them but we must also remember there are fights they have endured which we will never know of.

Betrayal

There are undertones in the life of every leader that must be understood when analyzing their makeup, things that are etched into the innermost part of their being which can affect their decision-making ability. Battles with beasts are one thing, but the betrayal of a loved one can leave indelible marks, as Samson would come to find out. Having won the battle with the lion with his bare hands, he would now have to fight the betrayal of his wife with his bare heart.

> *Judges 14:10 So his father went down unto the woman: and Samson made there a feast; for so used the young men to do. 11 And it came to pass, when they saw him, that they brought thirty companions to be with*

him. 12 And Samson said unto them, I will now put forth a riddle unto you: if ye can certainly declare it me within the seven days of the feast, and find it out, then I will give you thirty sheets and thirty change of garments: 13 But if ye cannot declare it me, then shall ye give me thirty sheets and thirty change of garments. And they said unto him, Put forth thy riddle, that we may hear it. 14 And he said unto them, Out of the eater came forth meat, and out of the strong came forth sweetness. And they could not in three days expound the riddle. 15 And it came to pass on the seventh day, that they said unto Samson's wife, Entice thy husband, that he may declare unto us the riddle, lest we burn thee and thy father's house with fire: have ye called us to take that we have? is it not so? 16 And Samson's wife wept before him, and said, Thou dost but hate me, and lovest me not: thou hast put forth a riddle unto the children of my people, and hast not told it me. And he said unto her, Behold, I have not told it my father nor my mother, and shall I tell it thee? 17 And she wept before him the seven days, while their feast lasted: and it came to pass on the seventh day, that he told her, because she lay sore upon him: and she told the riddle to the children of her people.

Many leaders do not go from glory-to-glory but battle-to-battle. When you love what you do and the person you love reciprocates that love, life is operating at peak performance. But when you love what you do and the person you love stops loving you, you begin to experience one of the greatest conflicts in life. As leaders we are accustomed to being in charge and in control, but when we cannot control the loyalties of those we love, it puts us into a tailspin as we attempt to process the betrayal of the beloved.

Just because a leader is accomplished does not mean they have mastered all areas of their lives. It would appear just because they can kill a lion, they should be able to control their relationships. However, love can make victims out of victors. Most leaders work hard, play hard and, I would venture to say, love hard. So when matters of the heart come into play, it can compromise the strength of a leader. This is why many leaders are public successes but private failures.

Sadly, in situations like these, we are quick to lay the blame on the leader for the failure of the relationship. Many times though, people connect to persons of subsequence for the wrong reasons. We see this in the timing: most leaders find love after their hair has grown in - that is, *after* they've been earmarked for success - making the motives of the beloved seem questionable.

Having to look over your shoulder for both beast and beloved is baggage leaders carry. They live with the possibility of betrayal from those they are betrothed to; and operate with skepticism concerning the people they are called to serve. This leaves the leader sleeping with the proverbial "one eye opened, one eye closed", leading their charges as "the bitter and the broken". When the closest ones to us are the ones who cause us the most pain, it is hard to lead without having a contaminated heart. I can wash the blood of the lion off of my hands but I cannot easily remove the brokenness of a shattered heart.

Consequently, divorce has become commonplace. It is something that happens when we fail to identify the calluses remaining on the hearts of those who have been victimized. It is difficult for us to imagine leaders as weak and vulnerable when they appear to be strong. But we must always remember, despite their achievements and accomplishments, they are anointed for "a thing" not "all things". Just because they fight well and fight often does not mean they always win. Many leaders are waxing cold because they are always under attack, be it from outside forces or internal confidants.

Is It Really Worth It?

Every leader has expectations of what it takes to defeat the lion but few have plans to defend against the betrayal of the beloved. Samson never trusted the lion but he did trust his wife. When you entrust the people who are closest to you to be the vaults of your valued secrets, you expect them to protect your interests. When the investments of the leader are devalued though, this causes the leader to question the value of leadership. Let us be honest: if the assignment has gotten us attacked in public *and* private, at some point we will begin to assess the value of the assignment. We start to ask, openly or privately, "Is it really worth it"?

Like David, nobody asked Samson if he wanted long hair. The anointing is heavy and sometimes too massive for even a leader of Samson's caliber to carry. But if we are to see our duty through, we must understand there will be times when the weight of the assignment will be far greater than the accolades.

Many people want to lead and to be in charge but they do not understand the strength it takes to carry something very few have ever borne. Leaders are an anomaly, not the norm. They must be able to handle the pressure of what they pursue. When they cannot, when they begin to experience a "bad hair day", they will seek to relieve themselves of the thing causing them pressure and pain. They will seek to get a haircut.

Delilah

In the book of Judges, Chapter 16, Samson discovers the one person who assists him in uncovering his true problem:

> *4 And it came to pass afterward, that he loved a woman in the valley of Sorek, whose name was Delilah.*

Contrary to how she has been portrayed in the past, Delilah was not Samson's problem: she was a symptom of the underlying issue and she would bring the thing lurking in the backdrop of his life to the forefront.

Every leader needs to identify their Delilah. To start with, she is acknowledged as "a woman in the Valley of Sorek". She lived in a lower place to Samson's higher place. Most leaders look for love on a lower level, where they can gain acceptance and affirmation. It is really an indication the leader has not matured beyond their lower place. When acceptance and affirmation comes from under you, it brings out the depravity that reigns in you. Delilah represents Samson's mindset: what you identify with is a reflection of what you are trying to suppress. You only fall in love with what is like you; and Delilah was an indication that something had gone gravely wrong inside of Samson.

Leaders must look at their selections to see where their struggles are and where they come from. Your choices are an indication of what you succeed or struggle with. Delilah is not the problem! The text specifically tells us that *Samson* loved Delilah, and as you lead, you need to be careful about who you love. Every leader needs to partner with someone who will bring out the best in them. Are you connecting the people who accentuate your positives? Or are you connecting with people who are trying to exploit your weaknesses?

An Enemy to Your Destiny

Judges 16: 6 And Delilah said to Samson, Tell me, I pray thee, wherein thy great strength lieth, and wherewith thou mightest be bound to afflict thee.

The problem for most leaders is that people want to connect with them based upon their gift and not who they are as persons.

People who wonder about your strength and not you, are an enemy to your destiny. People who try to uncover the secrets to your success without taking time to discover how to satisfy you are those who will be a part of your destruction. Remember Delilah was not *the* problem though she was certainly a *part* of it. She wanted to figure him out, to know what made him tick, but what she did not comprehend was that she was dealing with a ticking time bomb. He had been set apart to deliver Israel from the Philistines, but he himself had a burning desire in him to be delivered from the thing that made him different.

Leaders must become comfortable with “being different”. Like Samson, most leaders are not bad; they are just tired of being different. They want to be loved and still lead. They want to be first but still be part of the crowd. You cannot be great and normal at the same time though. There is an old adage that goes: “in order to lead the orchestra, the conductor must first turn his back to the crowd”. If you are not willing to be different and turn your back to those you are leading, then you need to know there is a Delilah assigned to you to make you just like everyone else. Most leaders believe they want to be normal until they have their encounter with her and leave her lap looking like everyone else. Then it is too late. But it does not have to be. If we could understand the things that lead us to Delilah’s lap, then we can avoid her altogether.

Tied Up

Judges 16:6 And Delilah said to Samson, Tell me, I pray thee, wherein thy great strength lieth, and wherewith thou mightest be bound to afflict thee. 7 And Samson said unto her, If they bind me with seven green withs that were never dried, then shall I be weak, and be as another man. 8 Then the lords of the Philistines brought up to her seven green withs which had not been dried, and she bound him with them. 9 Now there were men lying in wait, abiding with her in the chamber. And she said unto him, The Philistines be upon thee, Samson. And he brake the withs, as a thread of tow is broken when it toucheth the fire. So his strength was not known. 10 And Delilah said unto Samson, Behold, thou hast mocked me, and told me lies: now tell me, I pray thee, wherewith thou mightest be bound. 11 And he said unto her, If they bind me fast with new ropes that never were occupied, then shall I be weak, and be as another man. 12 Delilah therefore took new ropes, and bound him therewith, and said unto him, The Philistines be upon thee, Samson. And there were liers in wait abiding in the chamber. And he brake them from off his arms like a thread. 13 And Delilah said unto Samson, Hitherto thou hast mocked me, and told me lies: tell me wherewith thou mightest be bound. And he said unto her, If thou weavest the seven locks of my head with the web.

Leaders must identify the predicaments they place themselves in to recognize their hidden fetishes. In the scripture above, we discover Samson's vice: he was a pleasurable man. First he tells Delilah to tie him up with rope, then to weave the seven locks of his hair in a web, each incident appearing to be more painful than the last. This vice caused him to forfeit his destiny; and likewise, it is the "freaky things" in our lives that cause us to do the same.

Many leaders are so structured and disciplined in many areas of their lives, they allow themselves to be reckless and undisciplined in a few. In this circumstance, Delilah represents the ability to uncover the wild areas waiting to destroy our leaders. Samson's fetish took him down a path that kept him intimately connected to someone who sought to destroy him. No leader should ever confide in someone outside of their covenant.

When conversations shift to things that satisfy our flesh and do not fortify our purpose, then we are in a treacherous relationship. Delilah is extremely dangerous because she exposes our bend towards the carnal. She exploits the fleshly part of us and keeps us from reaching our supernatural potential. Through Delilah, the depraved and despicable parts of our character are exposed, and the issues that affect my character, erode my ethics and displaced core values are revealed.

Vexed Unto Death

Verse 16 is the key to the entire scenario; it would do every leader well to understand this passage.

Judges 16:16 And it came to pass, when she pressed him daily with her words, and urged him, so that his soul was vexed unto death.

She pursued him and provoked him to the point where he died before he ever laid on her lap. It was the disappointment of Delilah that drove Samson to a moment of discovery: he could not trust anyone. I believe it was at this point he concluded no one was worth the pain and suffering he was enduring; and in an instant of abandon, Samson committed "suicide". He intentionally took the opportunity Delilah handed him to divorce himself of the thing causing him the most difficulty.

I am sure it was with great pain and great anguish that he decided to sabotage his success. Samson did what we talked about earlier: he engaged in suicide by Delilah's hand. Just like the person who stands before the cop and gives them an opportunity to take their life, Samson stood before Delilah and allowed her to pull the trigger. I am convinced he could not understand or even wrap his mind around the concept of removing his hair with his own hand - few leaders are ever willing to cut their own hair. So Samson allowed Delilah to cut his hair.

Most leaders fail because they are tired of standing. They are so bent down by the weight and burden of their calling they look for a way out. You cannot quit so you get in a position to have the calling removed. Most leaders have not figured out a better way to stop being who they are, so they subconsciously sabotage themselves and have someone else remove their hair.

Samson was so disappointed, the Bible records he was literally vexed unto death in his soul. He was so wounded in the innermost part of his being; he believed his only recourse was to tell Delilah his secret. Samson told her everything, going back to where it all started in his mother's womb; and when you divulge to Delilah, she starts to divest you of your destiny.

Many leaders reading this book are people who have suffered a long time. They were great before they got their assignment, but they had to navigate the landscape of life for a long time and many of them have experienced more at an early age than most of us will in all of our ages. Most leaders have done a lot of living in a short amount of time; and the truth is a lot of them are tired. Never underestimate the power of simply being tired. Being tired brought Samson's fetishes to the forefront, causing him to forfeit his entire future. Being tired caused him to lay his head on Delilah's lap and allowed her to cut off the thing most significant to his existence.

Most leaders want to have an India Arie moment: "I am not my hair". But you are. As much as you want your long hair gone, remember, as the hair goes so do you. So do not let tired take you into the place where you sabotage your own success. Do not get so bogged down and burdened by people who are outside of covenant that they cause you to want to kill the thing you are called to do.

Suicide

Verse 19 is the place where many of you reading this book are living.

> *Judges 16:19 And she made him sleep upon her knees; and she called for a man, and she caused him to shave off the seven locks of his head; and she began to afflict him, and his strength went from him.*

After Delilah shaved Sampson's locks, the Philistines placed him in fetters and gouged his eyes out. Instead of escaping his bondage, Sampson found himself immersed in it. Now he was normal but blind. He was ordinary but bound by shackles; common, but imprisoned. Like Samson, you are in the place where your desire is to lay your head in the lap of the one who can relieve you of your burden. You close your eyes and go to sleep, as Delilah begins to shave your head. Now you *look* normal but you wake up to discover you have a greater dilemma.

Absent of their hair, many visionaries end up in the same position: blind, bound and living in a prison. As long as you had your hair, you could move beyond the internal, but now that you are normal your internal has become your external reality. Many leaders forfeit their reign only to end up in a reality that gives evidence to the hell they have existed in during their tenure. This is why it is best to keep your hair and be different. From your mother's womb you were set apart, so for you not to be different means there is no need for you to exist.

Samson went from compromising his gift to committing suicide, ultimately getting revenge on his captors in death (Judges 16:21-30) but I submit to you he did not have to die. Verse 22 states "the hair of his head began to grow again after he was shaven", but because Samson was blinded to his future, he opted to end his life instead. It is unfortunate that Samson did not receive the grace of regrowing his hair again. It was available to him, but he did not accept it. Every leader who has forfeited his identity and had his hair shaved; despite the blindness, the fetters and the prison, you can live again. There are times it seems easier to end it all and take out your enemy with your death, but who would be left to defend and protect those whom you were called to serve?

Regrowing Your Hair

Do not bow out because you are blind. God's grace has allowed your hair to grow again during your capture. The prison is an opportunity to reflect on the promise instead of the punishment. It is an opportunity to be locked down so your locks can grow back. Every leader needs distance between their destiny and the damage done so they can return to being what they have been. With all you have suffered from your moment of forfeiture, you need to discover how to get up and move forward in the gift God is giving you. Do not do a good act and substitute it for living out your God-given destiny. God never said there would not be ramifications for your actions but he did promise he would be with you all the way to the end.

Remember it was your hair that made you who you are, not your eyes. Every leader walks by faith, not by sight. As long as you have hair, you will be able to see, because you will be looking through the eyes of God; and as long as your hair grows, you can do it again. This is not your end! Do not be paralyzed by the pain of your past. Understand that beyond your problem, God still has a plan. Do not put your hand to the posts as Samson did; put it back on the plow.

As your hair grows out again, place your hands back on what God called you to handle. He is not counting you out because of your frailties. He understands the failures of the flesh. He factored them in before you began and knew there would be times you would want to divest yourself of what was invested in you. God is not intimidated by your temptation to remove your hair. He is not looking to take you out, so keep yourself in the game of life. Every leader at some point wants to be done with the thing that makes them different. It is in these moments of frail humanity we need to discover the power of a God who never gives up on the purpose he has placed within us. If Samson had rediscovered the beauty of being different, he would have never made the decision he did; he would have never chosen to die with his enemy.

You can either die in an arena or you can rediscover your purpose for being different and defend your nation. Which will you choose? God has chosen to allow your hair to grow again. When we stop fighting the plans of God and start to embrace his will, then we will stop allowing our resistance to take us to our death. It is better to want the will and the purpose of God for your life than to desire to have the acceptance of people who will take your life.

In verse 30, we read Samson's last words: "Let me die with the Philistines". His gift was given to defeat the Philistines, not to die with them. When the language of the leader changes to a declaration of defeat, it is an indication that death will soon follow. Do not die amongst what you were called to defeat. Do not die looking like the enemy. You were created to be different. Wanting to be like everyone else is the most self-destructive desire you could ever have. God wants everyone to know you are not like them. He uniquely qualifies and identifies you. You may walk amongst the people but at the end of the day, you still stand out.

PART III: ELIJAH AND ELISHA

Learned Behavior

Beyond the rise from common and desire to be normal, we need to address the relationship between mentor and mentee. We must understand what happens when leaders fail and pass on their failure. Much of the dysfunction that leaders deal with is learned behavior, which is reflected in the model of mentor and mentee through the established pattern of Elijah and Elisha.

Because it is extremely difficult for us to receive the inadequacies of the accomplished, many of the responses I receive when I talk about the flaws in the paradigm are raised eyebrows and confounded expressions. We want to see the genius in an individual or the depravity, but not both. It is problematic for us to reconcile within ourselves that an individual can be both great and flawed at the same time.

But this is contrary to what the Bible teaches us. This book was written for both admonishment and admiration, showing us the strength of its icons as well as their weaknesses. It is amazing how such a balanced book brings about one-sided viewpoints; and when we fail to see the totality of what the text desires to teach us, then we fail to glean all it has for us.

This is why it is so important for us not to romanticize the stark realities that reign in the life of iconic leaders. Elijah is a prime example: we only see his exploits and his accomplishments, but we are afraid to see his frailties and his inadequacies, as if they might undermine the greatness of his victories. A driving thought even in today's society, it is almost inconceivable that an individual can be a profound leader and an inadequate husband; a financial wizard but a poor father; an accomplished CEO of a Fortune 500 corporation but cannot keep their family afloat. As difficult as it is to fathom, you can be extremely accomplished in one area and be a total failure in another.

Unfortunately, many leaders are immediately discarded and disqualified because of their imperfection. It is the proverbial "throw the baby out with the bathwater" scenario. However, as we have already seen with David and Samson, much can be learned from a leader's failures. In Elijah's case, we do not have to undo the miracles he performed just because we find he was flawed, but we can accept that someone as anointed as Elijah can be both perfect in purpose and perfectly flawed at the same time.

Elijah may have been a premier prophet but he was a poor father/mentor in the faith. This statement is shocking for many because we have long heralded his connection with Elisha as the ultimate example of what a father/son relationship should be. Many of our teachings around mentoring and modeling come from the example of Elijah and Elisha. We often celebrate and salute the question Elijah places before Elisha, "what can I do for you before I am taken away from you?", lifting Elisha's response of "let me inherit a double portion of your spirit" (2 Kings 2:9) to soaring heights before riding off into the sunset, believing this is a hallmark moment. However if you trace the text from the original command given by God to Elijah on the mountain, in 1 Kings Chapter 19, we come to a different conclusion about the relationship these two men shared.

A Simple Question

1 Kings 19:9 And he came thither unto a cave, and lodged there; and, behold, the word of the Lord came to him, and he said unto him, What doest thou here, Elijah? 10 And he said, I have been very jealous for the Lord God of hosts: for the children of Israel have forsaken thy covenant, thrown down thine altars, and slain thy prophets with the sword; and I, even I only, am left; and they seek my life, to take it away.

The scripture opens up with a cowering and suicidal Elijah hiding from the wicked queen Jezebel in a dank, dark cave. This is not a fitting description or narrative for a wonder-working, supernatural, almost superhuman icon like Elijah. But the text goes to great lengths to help us understand the paralyzed place this powerful leader found himself in.

Having learned of the death threats made towards him, Elijah ran away. He arrived at the foot of the mountain, where he was asked a question: "Why are you here, Elijah?" This is one of the most profound and problematic questions posed to any prolific leader in pursuit of things contrary to his or her purpose. His response though is that of a typical, self-absorbed, self-conscious and self-centered leader: "I have been…" Rather than acknowledge his current predicament and admit he had lost sight of his purpose, he chose to answer from the perspective of entitlement and remind God of his past accomplishments. When we confuse our "why's" with our "what's", we fail to reach the conclusion that realigns us again with our purpose.

God gave Elijah the chance to ask for help to get out of the cave he found himself in. If you do not know how you ended up where you are, you need instructions to get back to where you came from. Most iconic leaders in this position do not know how they ended up where they are, but instead of asking for advice, they respond by reading their resumes and rehearsing their accomplishments. What you have done cannot get you out of the cave you are in though. If you are honest with yourself, those accomplishments are the very thing that drove you to where you are. When you do not understand that your greatest strength is also your greatest stronghold, you will find yourself like Elijah, cowering in a cave unable to answer a simple question. When we are so "accomplished", the simplest questions becomes impossible to answer.

In the Midst of Chaos

God now brings Elijah out of the cave on to the mountain and...

I Kings 19:11...a great and strong wind rent the mountains, and break in pieces before the Lord; but the Lord was not in the way: and after the wind and earthquake but the Lord was not in the earthquake. 12 And after the earthquake a fire but the Lord was not in the fire: and after the fire a still small voice...

Could it be the things we believed God to be in, perhaps he was not? Sometimes the earth is shaking, fires are burning and the wind is blowing, but God is not in any of it. We find God instead when we are in the midst of chaos and we choose to run to him. We put our faith in him and not in our fears. In a chaotic moment, when Elijah is consumed with fear and cowering in a cave, he discovers where his faith really is. What have you been doing that has the appearance of God, is making a lot of noise, creating a lot of smoke and breathing what appears to be the breath of God, but is not in fact God?

When Elijah finally heard God, *he wrapped his face in his mantle and went out, and still in the entering in of the cave (I Kings 19:13).* Many leaders, like Elijah, hide behind the thing they have been advancing with when they are confronted with their frailties. They wrap themselves in their mantles, their calling, their anointing...the very thing they are identified with. It is a powerful thing, but it will not protect you from the question God has posed to you, "Why are you here?"

Elijah tried hiding and so do we. The propensity of great people is to cover and conceal rather than expose and be healed. But God continues asking. At the entrance of the cave, God posed the question again to Elijah, *"what doest thou here Elijah?"* Elijah goes back to his original response, which brings us to one of the most sobering realities: we either failed to see or do not want to wish to admit the truth regarding the patriarchal prophet Elijah - he was unwilling to move past his prior success, preventing him from discovering his present predicament.

Replaced

When Elijah did not offer the proper response, God answered for him:

> *1 Kings19:15 And the Lord said unto him, Go, return on thy way to the wilderness of Damascus: and when thou comest, anoint Hazael to be king over Syria: 16 And Jehu the son of Nimshi shalt thou anoint to be king over Israel: and Elisha the son of Shaphat of Abelmeholah shalt thou anoint to be prophet in thy room. 17 And it shall come to pass, that him that escapeth the sword of Hazael shall Jehu slay: and him that escapeth from the sword of Jehu shall Elisha slay. 18 Yet I have left me seven thousand in Israel, all the knees which have not bowed unto Baal, and every mouth which hath not kissed him.*

Did you get that? God told Elijah, "Anoint Elisha to be the prophet in your room, your place, instead of you." Elijah was being moved out of position so Elisha could be moved in. He was being replaced. I like to say it like this, and many people take issue with it but suffer me my folly as I submit Elijah was fired on the mountain by God. You can romanticize it, state this was a future prophesy, say this was God's acknowledgment of what Elisha would become; however the text is clear: God was speaking in the present tense, describing a present reality. We can be a little more merciful and declare Elijah was retired on the mountain; either way, the mantle was being passed on to Elisha that day.

So Elijah came down from the mountain and found Elisha just as God foretold; but rather than anoint and pass on the mantle as instructed, Elijah *hurled* it at him (1 Kings 19:19). The original language states he *violently threw* his mantle upon Elisha. Frustrated with himself about past performances, Elijah took it out on his mentee who had nothing to do with the moment on the mountain.

The first interaction between Elijah and Elisha reflects the frustration of a father/mentor towards his son. Reflected in the action is an aggression that speaks rather to the regret Elijah felt for his situation and his assignment to prepare his mentee for his future assignment. So many sons/mentees are made to perform for the affirmation of the father though God has instructed the father to affirm the son. When God instructs us to anoint the next we need to embrace the beauty of being able to mentor our successor, not scorn it.

Your successor has been acknowledged by God and will be anointed by you to continue the work that your faith is no longer at a level to produce. It is better to take the time to prepare them to properly handle your mantle than it is to leave them to figure it out on their own. Many protégés have to waste time pursuing the people who could perfect them, and subsequently they end up with many of the same frustrations and failures as their fathers. This is why mantles are to be placed not dropped. Had Elijah followed the instructions given on the mountain, the mantle would have never been subjected to falling on Elisha and it would have never been subject to failure.

Fathered From a Distance

Many leaders fall because their mantle fell upon them. Had your father/mentor prepared you for the mantle and placed it on you, you would have never had to spend time figuring out how to fit in. Mentoring and fathering is intimate and interactive; it cannot be done from a distance. A leader cannot be fathered from a distance.

We have to do a better job at anointing and appointing rather than abusing and confusing those we are called to equip. Instead, too many sons/mentees are made to perform for what their fathers know God granted them. Are you making your successor pursue you? Are you handling them out of your frustration? Or are you preparing them based upon their assignment?

It is dangerous when the father knows what God has called the son to do, and they ask the son what they want rather than informing them what has been done. We could avoid many valleys if our fathers would simply have a conversation with us about what God said to them on the mountain top of their life.

Elisha, in many ways, is an indictment of Elijah's frailty. He handled his successor out of the weakness of his failures and made Elisha the heir to his death. He left his legacy to chance when he chose not to affirm Elisha. Risk your money and your business, but never your legacy. Your successor is not your competition. They are the ones who will build upon your foundation. Their success will be the continuance of your legacy; likewise, their failure will be the conclusion of your legacy.

While of earth, Jesus had to be affirmed by God in heaven. It took the affirmation of the father to activate the anointing of the son and the confirmation of the Holy Spirit to bring forth the mighty works of a sovereign Savior. If Jesus needed affirmation, ought we not as well?

Like Father, Like Son

If you have said lately, "I made it, they can make it too," you have a grave misinterpretation of what it means to mentor someone. The dangers of fathering your successor from a distance include having them mismanage their gift and repeating your mistakes.

2 Kings 2:23 From there Elisha went up to Bethel. As he was walking up the path, some small boys came out of the city and harassed him, chanting, "Go up, baldy! Go up, baldy!" 24 He turned around, looked at them, and cursed them in the name of the Lord. Then two female bears came out of the woods and mauled 42 of the children.

The mantle is for the miraculous, not the immature. Yet we read Elisha used the anointing to kill some boys who were making fun of his bald head. He bungled his second miracle because he was manifesting the frustrations Elijah carried.

As leaders we can come to different conclusions if we have mentors who are willing to teach us how to properly process our gift. We celebrate the double miracles Elisha performed but perhaps there would have been more had Elijah taken the time to properly train him and teach him how to handle them. We limit the possibilities of what people can do by not teaching them the proper maintenance, mentality and management of the mantle.

We casually remark that success is having a successor, and this is true. But how much investment have we made into the person who will perpetuate our purpose? I have watched so much greatness go in the ground and end because the individual did not know how to become eternal.

So maybe God did Elijah a favor when he acknowledged, “the journey is too great for you" (1 Kings 19:7). No matter how great we are, sometimes the journey is greater. It takes divine partnerships and people to perpetuate greatness. Some of us, however, have gone to the extent of our greatness. We talk about what we have done and what we have been; all while God is trying to give us an "Elisha" so we can live beyond our past accomplishments.

Imitation is the Highest Form of Flattery

It would do the father/mentor well to understand the son did not take his mantle; he simply wants to do what he has seen his father/mentor do. The scriptures show us the tense interaction between Elijah and Elisha: “What have I done to you, Elisha (1 Kings 19:20)?", Elijah asks over and over, leaving Elisha to justify himself again and again. There must be some semblance of satisfaction in knowing there are people who want what you have. Sometimes - not all the time, but sometimes - ambition is simply an acknowledgment of the mentee's desire to be like their mentor. The son/mentee is not trying to *outdo* the father/mentor but simply striving to be *as great as* them. Greatness has a way of agitating the greatness in others and conjuring up the idea that if excellence is before me in the personage of this individual, then certainly excellence can be in me.

The comfort level of the father/mentor in this situation is dependent upon their past performances: if their light is growing dim, like Elijah's was, then they will be intimidated by the shining lights of their sons/mentees. To this end, do not let your light be extinguished in the cave.

PART IV: NOAH

Epitaph

We move from Elijah and Elisha to Noah, who achieved the level of fame and renowned most leaders can only hope for – just to leave a sobering epitaph that exposed his failure as a leader:

> *Genesis 9:28 And Noah lived after the flood three hundred and fifty years. 29 And all the days of Noah were nine hundred and fifty years: and he died.*

Let us begin our dissection of Noah's leadership by examining this declaration: he lived three hundred and fifty years following the flood. This was a fraction of his full age, but for all the centuries of his existence, we are told he did nothing notable following the flood. He planted a vineyard, got drunk and experienced an inappropriate moment in his tent; beyond that, the sum total of his existence and his experience is summed up in this sentence, with nothing more to add about his exploits prior to his death. We will talk more about what happened in the tent but let us first uncover what did not happen after the tent: he did not build anything; gather anything; or grow anything. He simply existed; then he died. It is a sad state of existence when the man whom the Bible boasts about for all he did to redeem and rescue humanity from extinction fails to leave a legacy. His life ended abruptly, even before he ceased breathing, leaving instead an epitaph that summed up his existence by how many years he lived.

Many leaders are known for the one thing they did and the other things they did not do. Noah built the ark that saved mankind, but he was *only* known for that. There were no notable deeds that followed; no moving speeches or grand examples of the gifts he displayed. Will that be the conclusion of your testimony? Will people forget you after your failure? Will your legacy be defined by how long you lived after your greatest moment rather than the greatness still in you? We often fail to realize that for all God has planned for our lives, for every destiny decision made for us, we are still the ones who will decide if we move forward or if we die. Like Samson, we choose if we are going to commit spiritual suicide or if we are going to rise up from our failures and move past them. After all, failure is not fatal, but if we do not continue living, then it will be permanent.

The Flood

As leaders, we begin our assent by being assigned to do the impossible. Noah was called upon by God to build a boat that would house two of each species of animals because he was about to flood the earth. It would take him many years to complete this task and he would have to endure the ridicule of the people, but in the end, Noah, his family and his charges would be saved (Genesis

6:13-8). In this, Noah's function was dual: do something that had never been done and say something that had never been heard. Leadership sometimes makes you look and sound crazy. Because you are privy to plans that other people are not, this will put a rift between you and them, and will cause you to wonder whether you are crazy or not. It is one thing when others question your sanity, quite another when you begin to. But this is when you have to press through the doubt and the naysayers. Like Noah, when you forge into your assignment, you will begin to produce exactly what God has asked of you.

But be wary about letting your flesh grow after it. At the end of his assignment, Noah became a "vineyard planter" instead of a "boat builder": he fell prey to the proclivities of his flesh. The same hand that built the boat planted the vineyard. The same mind that received the strategy from God to build the boat was the same one that devised the vineyard. How can one be divinely ordained and assigned but still possess the propensity to lean toward things that should have died in the flood?

Let us pause a minute and look at the purpose of the flood. It was to purge and purify the earth of its impurities. Everything depraved was designed to die in the flood. There are floods in every leader's life that God sends to drown our flaws so they do not make it into our future. But many leaders like Noah have become proficient with smuggling seed: we carry seeds of our past into our future when they should have died in the waters.

Noah should have leaned towards his newly discovered dominant gift of building boats and rescuing humanity and not on his past experience of planting vineyards. Boat building is a laborious task that calls for us to follow the blueprint of God, but planting a vineyard is simple and sinful, allowing us to make our own plans and destinies. I asked how one can be divinely ordained and assigned but still possess the propensity to lean toward things that should have died in the flood. Genesis 7:23 reads, "And every living substance was destroyed which was upon the face of the ground," which means if Noah had not smuggled the seeds onto the boat that he would later plant in the vineyard, they would have died in the flood. What have you brought on your boat?

Impeding Your Legacy

The thing you carry over will cause you to linger in Genesis 9:29: *And all the days of Noah were nine hundred and fifty years: and he died.* You accomplish what no one else has only to do what everyone has to do…die. I do not know about you but I do not want to redeem humanity and save animal kind just to end up with the same legacy as those who did nothing.

But what is so bad about smuggling seed, you ask? How does this impede the progress of my legacy? Genesis 9:20 tells us: *And Noah began to be a husbandman and he planted a vineyard.* The keywords here are: *and Noah began to be...* It would seem after your greatest success you would want to continue building upon what you have done, but the problematic place for most leaders comes after their greatest success when they look to become something other than what they have been. Success would seemingly beget success but for some it is a set up for a great failure. Discover where your success lies and continue in it rather than feed your desire to produce something else.

Isolated, Intoxicated and Uncovered

Stay with God's idea instead of your own. What he gives you will save humanity, but the idea you give yourself will have you drunken and naked in a tent.

> *Genesis 9:20 And Noah began to be an husbandman, and he planted a vineyard: 21 And he drank of the wine, and was drunken; and he was uncovered within his tent. 22 And Ham, the father of Canaan, saw the nakedness of his father, and told his two brethren without. 23 And Shem and Japheth took a garment, and laid it upon both their shoulders, and went backward, and covered the nakedness of their father; and their faces were backward, and they saw not their father's nakedness. 24 And Noah awoke from his wine, and knew what his younger son had done unto him.*

Many leaders end up isolated from those they saved, intoxicated on the elixir of success and uncovered in their tent. Celebrating your success is not an issue; the problem with being intoxicated comes when there are people willing to take advantage of you because you are not in your right mind. Sobriety for a leader is success. Your right and sober mind is your God. Your drunken state only solicits the attack of sons who are perverted; and for Noah, the perversion of the son coupled with the proclivities of the father produced an epic failure.

What you plant will always put you in a compromising position. The Bible does not go into the illicit details of what took place in Noah's tent but we can infer from his response that something horrific happened in this moment of compromise. The frailties of the father were exploited by the devious desires of a depraved son. Not only do we have to contend with smuggled seed but we must also deal with sons who are full of sin *and* survived the flood. When you are in your most private and vulnerable moment, you must remain vigilant to the possibilities of perverted people around you. Just because you are alone and in your own space does not mean improper people do not have access to you.

Always live in private as if you are naked and exposed to the world. Nakedness is only a problem to those who are in the company of people who seek to capitalize on their moment. Refuse to place yourself in a compromising position, for when you wake from your drunken stupor you may have to curse that which you were called to love.

Die Right

It's amazing how a night in a tent can outshine the brilliance of your past performance. Critics reading this may argue, "Well, they can't write everything about Noah." My answer to you is, "No, but they can select what they say last about you." It will be how you are remembered from that point on. What will be the last account of your life? I often tell people I live right so I can to die right. I want my last memories to be lasting memories. Where you die matters! What people hear of you matters! Remember your next act could be your last. So let me ask you: where will you die? What will you be doing when you die? And who will be left to explain it?

These, of course, are not issues with Noah, but I wonder, what if he had died in his tent drunken and naked? Every leader's last exploit can be diminished by the next thing they explore. As a pastor, I travel a lot, and knowing I could die in the midst of any act I involve myself in helps me maintain my integrity. My family would be left to discover what I did, to defend it only to be destroyed by it. They would not only have to bury me but they would also have to bare the shame I leave them with. We have an opportunity to leave a legacy: will it be a blessing or a curse? Which will you leave?

Notice I did not ask what you did; the question is, what will you leave? Personally speaking, my hope is when a book about my life is written, they will have to keep adding more chapters to fit all my doings rather than coming to an abrupt conclusion because I did nothing beyond the one big thing that I was known for. I would hate to the save the world and lose myself.

CONCLUSION

The Right Answer

As I stated in the beginning, the right questions lead us to the right answers, and the right answers bring us to the truth…a truth that is often overlooked: failure is a part of success; and until we learn how to handle failure, we will not find true victory.

Answer these questions:

- Who is in your circle of accountability?
- How do we accomplish that which we have never done before?
- Which will reign in you when you have to choose between your divinity and your humanity?
- How does a successful person face the areas they are not successful in?
- How do I discover myself when I have always lived for others?
- What do you need to change in order to encourage a successful reign as leader?
- How much investment have we made into the person who will perpetuate our purpose?

A successful leader is able to set aside his common beginnings and act kingly. He is able to accept that he is different from the crowd and should avoid those who seek to get close to him just to discover the secrets of his success. He can accept when it is time to pass on the mantle of his anointing to his successor, and he builds a legacy that will live beyond him. Failure may come, but he is ready for it, because he has his eyes on the end goal.

How does a leader arrive here when they are disgraced, scorned, ridiculed and left to put their life back together - a life that, for all intents and purposes, on the outside appeared to be charmed? A life wherein one hears the worst of human behavior; maintains the integrity of the counseling one has rendered; yet in the leader's time of failure he is scorned by the very people he enlightened concerning the grace and mercy of a loving and forgiving God? The trappings of a perceived perfect life are, at times, the fallacy of public life in leadership and particularly ministerial leadership. Titles, positions, fame, notoriety, wealth, riches – none of these are a cure for a decimated spirit.

In leadership, a leader's heart tends to focus on the needs of everyone else, not just to the detriment of him (or her) self but to the people closest to them – family, friends and loved ones. The shame and embarrassment of private struggles revealed in a very public way, to a great extent, can be immeasurable when there is a public belief in ones' perceived perfect life. The immediate aftermath of the events surrounding a public "outing" are almost surreal, as if you are watching coverage of a person you barely know or recognize. A number of people may come to the defense of your "public self" because of the body of work you contributed to over the span of your ministry. To those who have the spiritual maturity to do so, a fallen leader is immensely grateful for the recognition of his life's work in context of the totality of that work.

A Line in the Proverbial Sand

The stark reality though is that a leader cannot have sustained excellence in ministry when leading from a broken place, nor should the leader be willing to lead from this place in his spirit. One has to draw a line in the proverbial sand and appreciate the intense scrutiny that comes in one's public and private life. We must live privately the virtues which we espouse publicly. Others might say you are an otherwise excellent leader and a "private life" matter should have no bearing on your ability to do your job. After all, *"we all sin and come short of the glory of God"*. And this may be an acceptable view of leadership from the outside; however, under no circumstances should the leader feel like the private "me" has no bearing on the public "me", especially when they are leading from a broken place that has not been dealt with or from a perspective of someone battling addictions and compulsive proclivities. Leaders constantly hear, "Talent can take you to places where only character is able to sustain you," and while this quote may be trite, at some point it has to resonate in the leader's heart and soul. A leader, particularly in Christian leadership, has to deal with their issues or eventually those issues will deal with them.

It is not the fall from grace alone which proves challenging; but the determination to get back up in Jesus Christ. A fallen leader has to ask himself, "Do I give up on me and give in to my acting out, my addiction, my compulsive behavior, or my proclivities which manifest themselves as sin? Do my good qualities and attributes entitle me to fall because of legitimate grievances in my life which have brought me to this fallen place in my life? Or do I hold myself accountable for my failures and start on the path toward redemption which is a long, tough, but necessary road?" The Bible, the very guide by which we preach, teach and live, is ripe with examples of failures in leadership and the redemptive paths these patriarchs and matriarchs took towards restoration to fully anointed leaders of our faith.

Until a fallen leader is able to truly feel the pain and devastation of their fall, there is a heartfelt, yet poorly executed vow to self-correct and inevitably the flawed leader falls into the same compulsive cycle.[1] Without honest self-assessment and strict accountability measures for the fallen leader, the desire to hide the proclivity can be much stronger than the will-power required to change the behavior that precipitated the leader's fall. Getting away with "it" is a powerful disincentive for tackling the tough work of recovery from sin[2].

---

[1] Acts 20:28 "Take heed therefore unto yourselves, and to all the flock, over the which the Holy Ghost hath made you overseers, to feed the church of God, which he hath purchased with his own blood."

[2] Galatians 6:7 "Be not deceived; God is not mocked: for whatsoever a man soweth, that shall he also reap.

Many times we loathe the thought of pain and disappointment, but they are very useful in our quest to be and get better. It may sound counterintuitive, but ponder this analogy: physical ailments are often preceded by some sort of pain, discomfort or symptom that will cause you to seek relief from the pain. Some remedies eliminate the ailment; others only temporarily relieve the surface issues of a much, more significant problem or disease. The supposition here is that absent of the pain, discomfort or symptom, our bodies will not know how or when to seek relief and help. Cancer of the pancreas is an insidious disease because by the time symptoms are present, typically the prognosis is terminal. Hypertension is known as the silent killer because it can go unnoticed. There are few if any symptoms that accompany the disease until it manifests itself as a heart attack, stroke or kidney failure.

A Living Example

In the same way, addiction, compulsive cycles, and a general, uncontrolled appetite for sin can be analogous to some of the diseases that show little to no symptoms. Most fallen ministry leaders who have successfully fought their way back, can say assuredly that in retrospect, the signs (loss of job, destruction of friendships and relationships, erosion of trust, etc.) had been present but there was not enough pain present to warrant the necessary effort to get "me" fixed. The desire to live in integrity and recognition of the contradicted existence of a fallen leader most often starts long before the most intense pain of the leader hitting "rock bottom"; however, once one has bottomed out because of a lack of recognition of one's own shortcomings; and is finally receptive to the requisite care and accountability needed to live a life of standard precipitated by that "pain", the prospects for living life in sustained integrity are very promising.

King David was a murderous adultery; Rahab was a harlot; Abram was a liar and demonstrated a lack of faith in the promise; Noah was a drunk; Moses was a murderer; Peter denied Christ; the Apostle Paul oversaw the slaying of Christians; and the list goes on. It is exhaustive regarding the shortcomings and failures of leaders who fell prior to and in the midst of their assignments. A fallen leader who is repentant does not display his failures as a badge of glory in pride, but as an example of the measure of the grace of God experientially and illustratively. The redemption story serves as a method to encourage the body of Christ; showing the leader's integrity is not limited to the conduct that precipitated his fall but to his ability to be restored to his anointed place through obedience[3] to the Word of God.

The sovereignty of God allows these low places in a leader's life to be used as a means by which to chasten the disobedient leader as well as an experiential method to take the stories of the Bible and give them present-day truth and life in the body of Christ. The

[3] 1 Samuel 15:22 "And Samuel said, hath the Lord as delight in burnt offerings and sacrifices, as in obeying the voice of the voice of the Lord? Behold, to obey is better than sacrifice, and to hearken than the fat of rams."

"Gospel According to…" is made alive through our testimonies of overcoming beyond the pages and letter of Matthew, Mark, Luke and John. The redeemed leader has a very unique opportunity to be a living example of the redemptive power of the blood of Jesus. If we were to look at the success of 12-step programs whether it be alcohol, food or sexual addictions, the power and success of the recovery programs is in the experiences – good or bad - of men and women who have had similar compulsivity's and challenges to maintain sobriety. Receiving the counsel of someone who has "been there and done that" is powerful to one who is seeking to overcome their issue. The living example of a transparent leader is much more impactful than a theoretical example of some of the iconic characters of the Bible wherein the "saved" derive their divine inspiration.

Growth

Perchance you have experienced failure. Like David you are reenacting the mistakes of your mentor. Or maybe you are contemplating spiritual suicide at the hands of your Delilah. Or perhaps you might be frustrated with your situation and are taking it out on your successor just as Elijah; or like Noah, you are not producing much of a legacy. These failures are real and relevant even today.

Failure is devastating yes, but it does not represent the end of your gift. It is only final to those who fear moving beyond it.

When we understand that it is factored into the equation of our success, we will not opt out at the first sign of difficulty. It can be our greatest teacher if we learn to view it as a tool for development and not the end of our assignment. We have all done things we are not proud of, things we wish were not part of the epitaph of our lives. But every great leader's response to failure should be growth.

My dad would always tell me, "Son, a mistake isn't a mistake as long as you learned something from it." Sometimes our greatest education is experience. It does not come from walking the hallways of a prestigious university, but from the tragedies we incur when we have the courage to try. Leading is a risk and with those risks come challenges that exceed our human frailty. When this occurs, the goal is to come out of the experience not unscathed, but having been made better because of it. If you are reading this book and you fall into the category of feeling like a failure, I am here to come alongside you and lift you to your next place of leadership. The same God that created you is still on the throne and has the power to re-create and build you up better than you have ever been.

The failure you experienced is not your end, but the beginning of a life that can shine more brilliant than it has ever shined. You just need to move forward. You may have fallen off your proverbial horse, but get up, brush yourself off, get back on and let us ride into the hope of a tomorrow that will be greater than your yesterday. Leaders fail, they just do not stay in that fallen state. They live out of their convictions and not their condemnation; and for this reason, I am here to speak louder than the voice of the experience that condemns you. I declare and decree to you that everything God placed in you is still there and will be utilized for his glory and the success of his people. Your failure is not final but will become a force that will flow through the earth and stand as the expressed image of Christ's love towards fallen man. Take your experience and your difficulties and wear them as a badge of honor, not shame. Share your tragedy and show your triumph so that others will know the redeeming power of our Lord and Savior Jesus Christ. You woke up today with an opportunity to get it right. This is what grace is – the chance for us to do things the way God intended them to be done. If you are reading this book, it is because God has graced you with another opportunity to get it right. Even with all of your missteps, mix-ups and mess-ups, God has been faithful. His faithfulness protects purpose and can move you past the proclivities of your flesh and the problems of yesterday.

Time to Heal

It is the breaks in life that make us better and stronger, but only if we set the bone and take time to heal. I played quarterback in my freshman year of high school. One day in practice, I missed the handoff during a broken play and was hit high and low. The next thing I knew I was waking up to a crowd of people standing around me. They tried to move me but my arm was dangling and my body was in indescribable pain – I had broken my shoulder. For six weeks, I slept sitting up in a chair, but I was not completely diligent about following my doctor's orders. There were times I would attempt to revert back to old habits like lying down, working out and maintaining the ways of life prior to my break. Needless to say, I was so excited when the end of my recovery period arrived. There were still some games left in the season and I was going to return to a starting position.

The big moment came when I went to the doctor to get my release to play. However, not only would he *not* release me but now there was talk about having surgery done on my shoulder because I did not take time to do what was necessary for it to properly heal. I pushed through the everyday pain, maintaining a natural routine, but I did not allow myself to properly heal. Consequently, the lack of attention to my injury created complications that have followed me through life. My movement prior to my healing caused the bone to shift and it grew back stronger but in the wrong position; and this strong, crooked bone had to be eventually removed to alleviate the constant pain I was suffering.

I have not played football since that day. A broken play led to a broken shoulder which led to the end of possibilities. Sometimes our eagerness to get back to our assignment pushes us past the opportunity to heal properly; but if we settle ourselves and take the time we need to recover, we can come back to the starting position and not have to deal with a career-ending injury.

For you, it is recovery time. Whatever the broken shoulder of your life, let someone set it, then follow the recovery instructions. It will be painful, and you may have to sleep sitting up for weeks, but the result will be a successful return. Painful things produce purposeful results!

Maybe it is time to stop healing others and start being made whole. As leaders we always qualify our success by our accomplishments, but we need to focus on our mental and spiritual health. Getting the job done is not as important as how the job is done. To heal others and not be whole yourself is what gets us removed from the team. Concern yourself with your health or like me you can desire a return to the game all you want, but because you are not healed, you will not be released to play.

Who You Are

Failure is a gift if we exercise our grace to grow through it and from it. It is the calcium of life that fortifies us, strengthens us and supplies power for the next phase of our journey. It affords us wisdom absent of the experience we would not have otherwise had. Failure is not a reason to quit; it is an opportunity to grow and discover who we really are.

One thing I discovered is you cannot keep a quitter from quitting and you cannot keep a winner from winning. The only thing you can do is delay the inevitable. A winner will win no matter what and a quitter will quit no matter what. I believe you are a winner and not a quitter. You did not get to this point just to give up. You made it to the mistake, but do not mistake yourself for a quitter. You have experienced loss before and recovered; you faced worse and came out better. Giving up is not an option as long as moving on is. Winning is what you do because it is who you are!

Let me remind you who you are before you allowed your failure to define you: the sum total of who you are is not the one shameful moment you may have experienced. There is more God in you than the bad thing you found yourself in. Recovery is part of his turnaround plan for your life and you can start today. You can live as if you never failed. Receive the grace of God and stop living as the fallen. God has forgiven what is hard for you to forget. He is faithful even when we are not. He sees you for what he made you to be and not for what you have done. Now "be" and you will not "do".

We do things we do not like because we do not know who we be. This statement is not grammatically correct but it is accurate by way of revelation. See yourself as God sees you and not how you see yourself. You will become the gift to humanity that God would have you to be and not the one who negatively impacts others. There is so much more to you than your shortcomings and your frailties. Remember failure is to train and develop you but it does not have the authority to define you. It may have been your schoolmaster but you are not its slave. Failure is a tool, not your tag; and while it is factored into your equation, it is not your final outcome. You have the name and the nature of success.

ABOUT THE AUTHOR

Since accepting Jesus Christ as his Lord and Savior, Pastor Ronald L. Godbee has pursued the mandate of God to seek and save souls through the preaching of the gospel. Pastor Godbee's greatest decision was first to choose Christ as his Lord and Savior; and secondly to choose Karla Godbee as his wife. Together, they are the proud parents of three lovely children Kindale, Ronald Jr., and Kharrington. After being faithful to his calling as a traveling evangelist, he established the Inner Court Christian Center in the heart of the inner city of Detroit, Michigan. With worship as its thrust and the love of God as its reason, Inner Court Christian Center impacted the lives of the lost.

During Pastor Godbee's time of ministry in the city of Detroit he was appointed by Presiding Prelate Bishop Edgar L. Vann II to serve as general overseer and executive Council member of the Kingdom Alliance Covenant Fellowship. Pastor Godbee has made many appearances on Christian television and has been a regular host on many Christian talk shows, including "Rejoice in the Word" with Bishop Greg Davis.

Pastor Godbee's transformative message, passion of worship and love for people has given him the touch of God for these times. He currently serves as the lead pastor of The River Church in Durham, North Carolina, which was established by

Bishop Joby and Pastor Sheryl Brady. He serves God's people with a humble and submitted heart; and is leading his church in becoming a model ministry of the 21st century.

Visit www.ronaldgodbee.net for more information; or email Pastor Godbee at ronaldgodbee@outlook.com.

52567876R10063

Made in the USA
Charleston, SC
17 February 2016